HoodWitch

HoodWitch

poems | Faylita Hicks

ACRE
CINCINNATI 2019

Acre Books is made possible by the support of the Robert and Adele Schiff Foundation
and the Department of English at the University of Cincinnati.

ISBN-10 (pbk) 1-946724-24-6 / ISBN-13 (pbk) 978-1-946724-24-3
ISBN-10 (ebook) 1-946724-25-4 / ISBN-13 (ebook) 978-1-946724-25-0

Designed by Barbara Neely Bourgoyne
Cover art: Tyrone Geter, *Bullseye*, Target Series, charcoal and torn paper, 40 in. x 60 in. x 3 in.

The press is based at the University of Cincinnati, Department of English and Comparative Literature,
McMicken Hall, Room 248, PO Box 210069, Cincinnati, OH, 45221–0069.

Acre Books books may be purchased at a discount for educational use. For information please email
business@acre-books.com.

For Carz

Black motherhood has borne the weight of centuries of disgrace manufactured in both popular culture and academic circles. A lurid mythology of Black mothers' unfitness, along with a science devoted to proving Black biological inferiority, cast Black childbearing as a dangerous activity.

—DOROTHY E. ROBERTS, from the introduction of
Killing the Black Body: Race, Reproduction, and the Meaning of Liberty

contents

THE THIRD RITE OF SMOKE

HoodWitch

About the Girl Who Would Become a Gawd

i

You must remember that you are a Gawd
it started, a coffee-rimmed face glowing
through the screen, crowning the bleached walls
of her tiny room in gold. *Let your fears go for now*—
but fear, an itch behind the left earlobe, irritates her
for the rest of the night. Makes her out of mind
& out of sight. Just another black woman
from the university; another know-it-all
woke-ass type. She been tryna get seen
without getting got. Wants to be
remembered, for more than
the ripped stitch of her first name—
thick with the acrylic clicks
of her momma's first honest prayer
ever written in ink. She needs
some protection. Murmurs
againagainagain: *Ancestors*
& so above, so below.
Coaxes sage to burn
while she rubs up
new dime-store candles
with her heavy
slick-oiled hands
before she restarts time
with a "5 Tricks to Master
Tantric Yoga"
YouTube video.

She a temple
but she still needs
to prepare the altar;

ask for guidance;
bend back to split
herself in half

& scream.

ii

No one knows she been grieving
                              via chakra & Grey Goose
                         via brick dust & busted nuts
            via the neighbor's expensive-ass designer blunts
                    via the Florida Water & the rain baths
               via the trap tracks & her sister's strut line

she been screaming
    with her back snapped & flexed.

She been grieving ever since
    her momma explained that she is
                         part black woman, part hoodwitch,
                part *six-foot-three Caucasian,* part South Side,
                    part black-eyed peas, part bibliophile,
            part daddy between the legs, part mommy in the chest,
                    part cap & gown, part black hoodie.

She is
    all fear in the body.

iii

for years   she handled the trigger
like the tail of a fish   clenching the raw meat
in the bowel of her mouth   desperate not to swallow

or release the bullet   that cradled her in her sleep

followed her through the grocery store   bought her a drink

dusted up her sidewalks   stood next to her on the bus   left a wet place

   in her bed

where what she wouldn't do   to get away whole   left her split & seeping

she always knew   a single *Hey! Yo' ma!*

would translate her   into faint traces of her

shea butter &   argan oil

i

on the   W

d

n

iv

[7]She became a Gawd[8]under his body, with his weapon pissing iron into her[9]dark & saturated construction.

[10]Though it was not the Gawd anyone expected or the Gawd that anyone wanted—a Gawd born of electric heat & black pepper—[11]it was the Gawd that the world deserved[12]& in her making, sparks skid along her jaw, light trickled through the creased lip of the car's window [13]as she hollered in automatic clips;[14]a levy of time evacuating her body,[18]coating the lemon painted gutters of a nameless street in the rouge of her saffron-tinged tea, dripping through & down the passenger door.

[19]In his hurry to see her asleep,[20]the mess of her[21]marked the pink threads of his palms with the last notes of her foreign psalm[22]hyphenated by the beat of her breath— [25]became a bop unfamiliar to his neck,[23]hitting him like the curse it was,[24]plunged down to swell quickly [25]in the root of his left sole before it swam back up the path of his rod, twisting at his cords quickly slit against [26]her final prayer.

[27]The year mothered another blood moon tribute. [28]*What else was I supposed to do when an animal came looking for me?* he later asked the officer,[29]gazing over at the blaze—to where the fire was now lit—[30]withering & wondering[31]at the ecstatic leap of Her reaching flame.

#SayHerName#SayMyName#SayHerName#SayMyName#SayMyName#SayHerName#SayMyNa
#SayHerName#SayMyName#SayHerName#SayMyName#SayMyName#SayHerName#SayMyNa
#SayHerName#SayMyName#SayHerName#SayMyName#SayMyName#SayHerName#SayMyNa
#SayHerName#SayMyName#SayHerName#SayMyName#SayMyName#SayHerName#SayMyNa
#SayHerName#SayMyName#SayHerName#SayMyName#SayMyName#SayHerName#SayMyNa
#SayHerName#SayMyName#SayHerName#SayMyName#SayMyName#SayHerNamc#SayMyNa
#SayHerName#SayMyName#SayHerName#SayMyName#SayMyName#SayHerName#SayMyNa
#SayHerName#SayMyName#SayHerName#SayMyName#SayMyName#SayHerName#SayMyNa
#SayHerName#SayMyName#SayHerName#SayMyName#SayMyName#SayHerName#SayMyNa
#SayHerName#SayMyName#SayHerName#SayMyName#SayMyName#SayHerName#SayMyNa
#SayHerName#SayMyName#SayHerName#SayMyName#SayMyName#SayHerName#SayMyNa
#SayHerName#SayMyName#SayHerName#SayMyName#SayMyName#SayHerName#SayMyNa
#SayHerName#SayMyName#SayHerName#SayMyName#SayMyName#SayHerName#SayMyNa

black girls who knew the scent well—
rushed home to oil their scalps & deep condition

01110011 01100001 01111001   01101000 01100101 01110010
01101110 01100001 01101101 01100101

01110011 01100001 01111001   01101101 01111001
01101110 01100001 01101101 01100101

burn wick & conjure hell

#SayHerName#SayMyName#SayHerName#SayMyName#SayMyName#SayHerName#SayMyNa
#SayHerName#SayMyName#SayHerName#SayMyName#SayMyName#SayHerName#SayMyNa
#SayHerName#SayMyName#SayHerName#SayMyName#SayMyName#SayHerName#SayMyNa
#SayHerName#SayMyName#SayHerName#SayMyName#SayMyName#SayHerName#SayMyNa
#SayHerName#SayMyName#SayHerName#SayMyName#SayMyName#SayHerName#SayMyNa
#SayHerName#SayMyName#SayHerName#SayMyName#SayMyName#SayHerName#SayMyNa
#SayHerName#SayMyName#SayHerName#SayMyName#SayMyName#SayHerName#SayMyNa
#SayHerName#SayMyName#SayHerName#SayMyName#SayMyName#SayHerName#SayMyNa
#SayHerName#SayMyName#SayHerName#SayMyName#SayMyName#SayHerName#SayMyNa
#SayHerName#SayMyName#SayHerName#SayMyName#SayMyName#SayHerName#SayMyNa
#SayHerName#SayMyName#SayHerName#SayMyName#SayMyName#SayHerName#SayMyNa
#SayHerName#SayMyName#SayHerName#SayMyName#SayMyName#SayHerName#SayMyN

The First Rite of Water

Wolf

I found her naked,
arms wrapped around
a photo of us; candle wax
in the carpet, shards of light
cutting into her brown skin.
Last night the walls bled. *God*
came up in the house, she said,
was in our adjusted periphery
& in her legs. Dropped a drum in her.

She a Wolf now. She say
I ate the moon whole. She's full
of brooms & weapons now;
sweats like a pit bull. She can smell
the shit on me now. She says
I finally found a way
to clean the blood
out the carpet. Gets down
on all fours—starts licking.
She says *I a Witch*
now. Can't nobody break
what's broken & I'm all ivory
now. She warn me to get gone.
She can see the devil itch
in a man's skin now.
She say *they gonna know*
I'm a Beast now.

My Sister has got a new
video online of Her panting
Touch me again & I will
tear this motherfucker down.

Ultra Sounds

They say *You have got to*
know when to cut & we women—
we black women—we've got to
do all the cutting ourselves.
Reach down.   *Push.*   Then pull.   & cut.
They say *The wound will heal, the sleeve*
is elastic & *isn't it beautiful*
what you've done, but we women—
we black women—don't feel
things like the rest of them. We women—
we black women—wear our ruin
out into the world, in gowns
of crisp white sheets
from our hospital beds; fashion
earrings from the empty tubes; cut
headwraps from the dirty pillowcases;
glue empty medical charts sharp
to the tips of our nails; pose in latex
gloves for the gram. In the light of
Saint Serena, we never play their games
but find ourselves in viral videos, planking
in the doctors' lounges, in their poorly lit lobbies,
in their parking lots, in their jail cells,
in their ambulances, on their operating tables.
We women—we black women—harvested
too soon & with little care. They say
that when women—especially the black ones—*feel,*
it is always too much; *just dying for attention.*
They say that we women—especially us
black ones—just need to learn how to *relax & live a little.*
More blood than bone, they say I ought to be more
sacrificed. Whatever I do, I should never be
The Wreckage.

The Birth Mother's Red Bath for Courage

With spoiled milk seeping
from its many small brown mouths,
my body twitched loose the dead
skin snaked around it, dripped
runes in the doorway,
heaved bullet after bullet
into the tub—but did not die.
There are claw marks
& hot grease stains
where things came through.
Signature survival signs
etched around my belly—
at the hinge, in the crevices.
All of it evidence: I did give birth
to something. There was a killing here—
of a kind. Something is lost now,
forced from a room in me. Something
is stifled in this body; I have become
a deconstructed basket
of rose-colored towels
singing on the hospital's floor.
Some nights, I think this body
must still be calling out to the child
that tore through it or trying to
forgive itself for giving itself over
to the strange & inconvenient truth
that not all mothers—are mothers.
Some mothers are war—an enemy
of their own desires. Some mothers
are graveyards—a field of want
buried beneath other fields of want.
Some nights, I think this body
must still be praying to a god
that has long since slithered away.

Photo of a Girl, 1985: Sistah

Gardena, California

Crowned in ruddy night-shades
& wet feathers, blessed by the blood
of my mama's only entrance—
I am a *sistah*. Her first-born
sacrament—to be consumed
& I know it & she knows I
will ruin her; teaching her
the art of mothering
a broken heart
in the shape of
a black girl;
a riot of fists.
An engine
caked in robin-
bleached lapels & token
posies, protesting: the svelte jaw
of the camera,
the mane of light
trying to suck me in;
the undeniable wound—
wicked at the crux of me.

Gawd

Womxn are the actual root
of all things. We are

the only ones   p u l l i n g   anything
out of our actual bodies.

The universe is a womxn
like god (or Gawd) is a womxn

& not God   not like man.
Gawd is a black womxn, the femme

body in blxck—come to take back what was theirs:
the universe & everything in it.

For the sake of balance, Gawd
is a body that knows

no boundaries.

Photo of X, 2003: Abstractions

Austin, Texas

What goes on & on & on forever with no clear beginning & no clear ending? Death & did I start to die before I was even born or was I born & then I died & is it death if I've never lived? At what point has death begun & at what point is it over? Are we always dying or is there ever a safe space for universality: an always? A woman's strength is sometimes rooted in her humility, sometimes in her Gawd. Sometimes it is a body familiar with bloodletting, familiar with letting blood empty itself from the body. Sometimes a woman's strength is rooted in her joy, if joy is a knowing that life is finite. Her joy is knowing that she could be as unborn & erased as those before her. Sometimes strength is rooted in a body that is neither of the sexes. Is it sex, then, that roots us in the bodies of others or is it blood that roots us in the bodies of others & must we be in the bodies of others at all? *Aren't we always in the bodies of others dying to be released or is release the fallacy?* Are we always attached to a body or are we more than our bodies? Are we weighted into our skins & waiting to be released? Is release really a release, if we are always living in the bodies of others as blood? Is my blood *my* blood if it is also my mother's & also my father's? Is my father a man or is he more than a man if he is also his mother's blood? Is he a wisdom? What is a wisdom if it isn't a knowing passed down through the blood, if it isn't my ancestors trickling down into my sheets when I'm asleep letting blood? Do you think we could be more than our bodies? I think I am more than this body. I can hear my grandmother calling me all sorts of names. I can see the backs of my grandfather's hands in my hands. If I follow the creases of my palms, it leads me to a mirror with my daughter's face in it. If I have a daughter, is she a universe? Does this mean my son could not be a universe? Even if he tried? Do sons carry universes inside of them? They must carry something because I could not create the universe by simply rooting myself in myself. I let sons root themselves in myself all the time & we make universes with our wisdoms, using the first law of thermodynamics, which is to say that our energy roots itself in the bodies of another & never dissipates & never is like Death in that it has no clear beginning & no clear ending 01100001 01101101 01101001 01100111 01101111 01100100

14

Photo of a Girl, 1988: Cyborg

Somewhere, Carolina

Standing next to my Momma, I mimic
the exposure of internal systems, revealing
an elegant smile creased white in the brunt of my dark face,
blue grease slipping down the side of my neck.

My sister coils around her leg, a frame
bent by mistake, & together we are
tint against the grill of the bleeding
velvet hood of a trifling sun-licked Corvette.

Momma poses with Her hips jut out,
with Her flesh-eating ammo
gossiping beneath the floral print
about the irony of carrying

a loaded whistle, hustled down
between Her copper rings,
& Momma *slash* Qween
is hype next to the hissing machine

She will later use to drive us over
to Jesus & back to Cali & down
to Texas &&&& to drive
my daddy's specter off

a murky dirt road & over to the other
unmarried piston-husked men &&&
back to my hologram of a daddy
with his lead-filled heart *slash* tongue

& I know what I am & will always be—
something that can & will survive
a whole century of hunt.

GrackelBot

In spits of feather & bone,
we grew with our chins raised
& our mouths propped open,
waiting for Momma to get off
from work, to make it safely home.
A faucet of wires, She would
sometimes trip
over our daddy's unfamiliar body—
once buried in the fatigue of war
but now raised & knocking
alwaysalways on our front door
like the automatic deliverance of a god
none of us young knew to know.
In those days, my sisters dangled
from my waist & I bruised black
from their peckings, bristled at
their hunger because I knew only
one conjure: that of light.
I flickedflicked airwaves
on the magic box & summoned
clues to happy endings via the Disney
Channel, bristled at the deluge of white
bodies gyrating in synchronized solidarity.
Such a strange concept, my sisters & I
took the TV apart; shoved the screens
down our throats & wondered—
what would happen
if we learned to glow
in the dark?

My Mother, the Forest

[1]My Mother, the Forest, whispers with the owls[2]about the true nature of men. The honesty of murder. The certainty of death—the necessity of it. [3]All day & all night, She hums about the bones of the red wolves buried somewhere beneath Her floor,[4]the children She never intended to hold on to.

[5]My Mother, the Forest, stacks up dozens of years as though they were axes. There, then, is where some went & never returned. [6]Some dreams & some children She never intended to hold on to. [7]I carry these slack-necked dreams like infants,[8]dragging their tiny breaths between the pines, from one dirt floor to the next. [9]The blxck body of every misshapen thought as heavy as a face with too many names. [10]I carry what's left of blxck girls along the familiar path;[11]a circle of time. [12]Knowing that beneath this consecrated ground—[13]beneath the birch trees, next to the pond, in the wood & under rock—[14]there is the spoil of blood. Beneath others' others—[15]their lies, the truth—those that we know[16]She killed with Her own greedy hands when She was young & mad.

[17]My Mother is sick with light—with Her fertile hunger for a god outside of Herself. [18]My Mother, the Forest, has become a green host to white men who lean out of rotting pines & pat their tight chests;[19]who whine about the loss of equality; who called my sister out her name; who asked her about: her dogs, her honey, 1985, & the quality of the local game;[20]who grabbed their groins & said they liked her gap tooth & knew where to find her missing daddy;[21]who whistled *ghost* & something about her shame beneath.

[22] My Mother, the Forest, sings *I am all bones with men dangling from my teeth & the ropes between my pines, beneath my birch trees.* [23] *They swing around the path of my neck now & no—I think nothing of them.*

[24] *Don't worry, child. They god could never save them now.*

Photo of a Girl, 1992: Gremlins

Somewhere, Carolina

Where I first learned to collect dirt—the graveyard
surging with the effigies of women forgotten or drowned
by the strange tide of hours flooding their small & empty
beds; blistered with the ghosts of their men trapezing
through the yard in the shoulders of their children; where
the army wives were hungry for large & hard
harbors or homes with cornerstones—anything permanent;
where Momma leaned against the double-wide & *S* posed
Her back; where chain-linked to Her homegirls, She posted up
against the slim carcass of the trailer She once roach-smoked
while She was out getting Her babies baptized
in North Carolina's largest pool of spousal ejection: Fort Bragg;
where scoops of women cocked back their glorious rounds
& checked their spines in a honeycomb of fatigued men;
where us grassy kids trained muddy snapping turtles
to be combat ready, chucked grenade-shaped pinecones
over concrete lots, & touched each other under our houses.
Back when I never knew what sort of work my Ma did
but I did know that whatever it was required She unzip Her skin
at the end of the day & paw a Kool cigarette between
Her fingers to let steam run through Her dank lips,
up & out into the facade of a clear blue sky; when She was shady,
just like the panther stalking up the plank of Her calf & digging
into Her plump waist; when I learned to say *Daddy* whenever
She said *Daddy*, when his face switched texture & tone—
depending on the shape of the moon; when I learned
it was only a phase, listening to the shallow waves tapping
against Her bedroom door whenever my father finally found
his keys; whenever my Momma remembered what love tasted like
when it wasn't salted with the solitary years of being a war's wife;
back when my Momma said I was too young to recognize *DANGER*
when *DANGER* followed; when I climbed onto the couch

& tried to revive Her late in the morning or tried to catfish her animal onto a paper plate or into a bowl or *something*, 'cause we were hungry; when *DANGER* fed my sisters & I: Cocoa Puffs & baloney sandwiches & count down to the days—*dammit*—until we finally got up out Her house & went on & raised up little gremlins of our own.

Photo of X, 1997: Something Not Right

Fort Hood, Texas

I had been wondering
if I was a girl or a boy
or just broken,
reaching down into myself
with a marker.
Fix yourself.
Momma found me
nagging a dictionary
& She came—a yawning
beluga whale, self-launched
into the air—Her nightdress
a white flame pushed up against
the flaps of Her breast.
Momma came for me.
Her lopsided curls garden snakes
unraveling as She flew
from my door to myself
& the puddle I made
with my questions on the floor.
She screeched & a leather face—
like a strip of land—kissed
my neck. Assuaged my back.
Bitter. Tight. Nicked the peach
behind my knee. My skin
hushed itself into a hum of red
& it was the first time
I considered bleeding beautiful.
I said: fix yourself.
But She had to know.
There was no fixing myself now.

Coded Binaries

For the work
of my wayward body
which is not myself
but is a vestigial structure—
they have determined
that I am confused or upset
with my Mother, angry
with my father,
& so *fuck him*
has become a man
sinking inside
of another man
whose body whistles
like mine; has become
a disciple's daughter
praising the work
of another woman
who may or may not be
another womxn—
who could be
a whirlpool of memory
dressed as a woman.
I have become
a station of ideas
salivating between
the legs; a fat-handled tool,
combing seasons, dragging flesh
from one shore to the next,
picking out reasons to live
after all that was done
to make me anything else
but real. I am the shadow
trailing the core of time,

half-alive with the wonder
of love in all its forms.
My father wished me son
& so I was.
My Mother wished me wise
& so I was.
I wished me whole & here
& so I am;
asterisk of the sun,
hyphen of the moon—
a wolf
in couture & candlelight
running between
the slack of their body,
summoning *Gawd*
with wrist & weight,
my mouth & mewing.
Had my love been
a single digit,
it would have settled in
as dust upon the altar,
but instead
it burns & burns
as wick—
hotter & hotter.

Photo of X, 2004: Fish with Yemayá

San Marcos, Texas

She lays me on the coffee table—like a bag of oranges fresh from the farmers' market. Opens me without bothering to wash me off or peel the labels. She digs Her fingers into my hair & pushes until I pull apart beneath Her, sighing as I cry on Her lap quietly; as much as is required. How She kneads me between Her lips; how easily against Her tongue I round & fracture—a slight exhaust of woman. Naturally. There is a ringing in Her cavity, not exactly citrus, but what is left of me sinks into Her damp, rough swallow & I am convinced to stay. I can watch the kitchen burn from here. I can listen to the skillet spit, hiss & holler from the pyre for: kosher salt, cilantro & lemon. I can consider the weight of Her peppered hands as they swell against the heated wood of my back. Conjure cayenne & butter & cumin in my pot. It is easy now to unravel under the return of Her mouth to my burning neck, roll my eyes back to the kitchen on fire & listen to my body take Her:

An open space of fresh saltwater.

Photo of a Girl, 1994: Gawd

Long Beach, California

I watch the flood splash & truck
by my first-floor window

before I see Gawd strut by
with Her Iron & Forty Ounce.

A wave of bodies—glittering onyx—catches air,
dips & weaves past the sill like a river of flies

that splinters at the sight of Her.
A legion of black ants

tripping down the street,
screaming *RUN*

as Gawd pulls a hammer—
whips spiders all through my kitchen.

Hoodies scatter into side streets
as Gawd saunters by

in Her slapping-pink slippers & creamy silk boxers—
unhinging. Reminding them

who they fucking with. Gawd heard *Samson
got his dick wet*—ships black hail

into my living room. Gawd says She's gotta
knock that shit out—hawks a bullet

into my bathroom. *Gawd*—I think—
Samson better get his ass out there.

*Gawd about to break Her neck on me,
looking for a little Gawddamn justice.*

A Note to My Daughter about Water

Full of stones & onyx knuckles,
       I am the tide that came for you.
      I am the wave—not a wound,
not an oven or even a mother
   now but—I am the one
      who made you. Think of the other
        ways that I have lived—softly
salted & quick. This is the true
     root of you, the skin of it:
   with my fingers around your throat
you grew. In the chop & crash—
in the rumble—you grew
    & now I will live forever.
       The root of my paper-mache kisses
& my origami lovers? Your mother's mother.
     Child, I came through her—
  too quickly—
       like you.

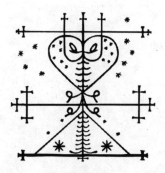

The Second Rite of Flesh

Photo of a Girl, 1984: Senior Photo
Compton, California

Trace amounts of Cali sun dangle
from my mother's teeth, her hair
levitating up over the crisp round cut
of her shoulders, the early hour carving
through her body still coveting saltwater
air & honey. A mourning aubade, she glows.

In the distance, men can be seen running—
a carousel of terrified ponies—chasing
each other out of the frame. A network of skin,
distilled by the sudden glint of her butane-
streaked face; their static insanity captured
forever in digital threat; their bodies convulsing
in a pixelated shudder as my mother throws
her neck back & laughs—fire slinging
from her throat, smoke detangling itself
from her eyes still reaching out to grab & eat
the camera.

The Kardashian Curse

The tintless women here
Mind my pockets; task me
For my thick hide & tight cunt;
Praise my gauze-trapped orgasms;
Envy me the herd of men
Who climb up out of me;
Crawl into the beds of my boys
& sickle my sons with their thirst;
Scrape me of my contour
& throw what's left of my body
Into their mirrors; stitch my name
Into the roofs of their mouths
So they too can #drippp
Authentic power; praise me
For my discounts on IG
But disbelieve
My lack of security; I'm lit
Oil in they pipes—a nova
Out of fashion with the times.
They don't love me as much
As they love the way I am
When I am smoked
& ghost drawn; I is
They idol until neon-
Stenciled skies hollow me
Like the gun clips
Of hook-handed fellows
Who hollowed me & holla my name
Under disco-chipped stars
With the same glow
As my vintage angles
& savage pose—I'm sick
With the light

Trapped inside of me
When they aside me; I am the closest
They've ever come to Gawd
In the flesh & yet they still
Have the nerve to take them fresh
"Brazilian" waxes to the center
Of South Shore, where they will swipe right
Until *Around what time*
Do you want to hook up;
Cast themselves in shades
Of bronze for bags & bills
Already paid—which, true,
Wouldn't be that bad
If only they didn't:
Jerk their necks like me, snap
Their fingers like me, squat pop
Over piles of money
In the shape of a TV producer
Who just happens to know
The true value of ~~false~~ b/ l/ a/ c/ k pain;
Shadow dip themselves
In my hustle & use my Gawd-
Given name in vain.

whoever.

The sweetbread of your figure is smeared in my *Screw Me*-red lipstick,
soaked in stale beer & stretched out on the spoiling linoleum—
not on my Egyptian cotton or the dingy hallway carpet
where I normally find the carcasses—but I assume it was you

who carried me home. I can't remember where I met you
or your name but you—you were good. Familiar almost.
Last night you were this awake yet à-la-carte kind of moment.
A reminder of things I've had stolen or lost somewhere along the way.

I remember—we were brilliant, fluorescent. Our figures splitting
contaminated light in our broken mouths every time we came on chorus.
That I remember. How we ruined the after-day this way:
with your cockings, the ticking of my ass against the ruddy counter

like a resonant slap against the faces of our Christian mothers
& all their Bible stories about Ruth & Boaz. I was waiting for you.
That I remember. Even though I knew that this could never be
a love story. Not a making of.   A killing.

Photo of a Girl, 1991: Hunt

Fort Bragg, North Carolina

a husband trails a wife pursuing a husband
on a sable night wrapped around
the frozen bodies of their girls.
a woman sprints from her husband.
a man gallops from his wife.
a cerise corvette chasing a nutted-brown chevy
through a trailer-park hive & past a double-wide
where their children sometimes play. around & around
where the switch grows thick & emerald on bushes
just outside their door. next to where a wife buried
her last tray of cigarettes & her twenties & her heat.
a husband buried his last bottle of ol' e & his fists
& his forgiveness. where their children fall asleep
to the lullabies of roaches fucking.

+

next night mama sniffs our front door.
sniffs her ratty sheets. flips our couch. turns
a tv box on. daddy growls out in the yard.
charges our front door. howls & howls. turns
an engine on. mama says *watch your*—stops. turns
an engine on. growls out in the yard.
a dirty hazel truck blazes past a crimson car
& out the trailer-park hive & past us girls
who sleep for years. wake to find muddy paw prints
under our sheets. tire tracks on our carpets.
cars still chasing trucks still chasing cars.
blind wheels still catching whiffs of salt & blood.

The Battered Woman's Prayer for Power

I have always known I was pivoted then crushed
against the fleshy shore of my own name. A breast

made of shrapnel moans. Consider the aggressive *Yes*
benign now in this body—a testament of my audacity

to exist at all. I have always known I was a wishing well
of a woman. A wailing wall of a woman. I am pound for pound

every bit an echo of the god I was before
I became what I am now. Now I am a critic

of the climax & of the breaking of this body.
Here, do this in memory of me: howl

when he knocks against your belly with his teeth,
when he threatens to carve you as anything less than glorious,

as anything other. Warn:
I will not go easy. There will be no victory here.

The Fantastic Life of My Guardian Angels

The angels followed me out of the church
down to the crossing of Riverside & Pleasant Valley
& down to the bowel of East Austin, into the zodiac-
crested buildings of an ancient hippie cemetery
also known as the Metropolis Apartments:
the last freestanding rebellion against the onslaught
of gentrification this far south in the city.
They were there with their hacky sacks at the ready;
propped up against the gates, their pearly wings covered
in a week's worth of travel & braided to the ends
with cotton candy beads; glitter dusting the high vogues
of their perfect cheekbones & pouty lips, rainbow halos
'round the new piercings riddling their new bodies.
Together, we templed to the faux DJ's music. Calling & casting
away with our hips the disciples we discovered
in this small, forgotten corner. Beside me, they thrust
their chests in suggestive, offbeat movements hyphenated
with humanlike hunger—begging for love with their gut.
When the rains came, I would rush to slide barefoot
through the mud of the courtyard's untilled lot, a fish in a pot
full of misguided millennials parlayed between youth
& scientific realities. Most afternoons, the angels hung over
the railings right outside my apartment door, flirting with the never-ending
partygoers & drinking fermented juice from the neighbors.
Most evenings they lay beside me, with their backs flat
against the jagged cement-slab floors, & we discussed
the spirituality of sex while grinding bud & posing.
One would pucker their lips & trick light into the bowl,
the other sashaying from one end of the hall to the other,
their shadow flipping birds into the cracked mirrors
of the sky-stained bathroom. All of us rude or elevated
on the nights we planned to go out. I considered moving only
after I had to hide the angels in my closet, the day that Young God

came through: a lost boy who bent me over & gave me prophecies.
Gurl, you could save me from the hurricanes of Louisiana
if you tried, & from the ghosts who followed.
I didn't think I could—the angels didn't think so either,
smirking at the cot I called a bed for seven months;
giggling & scribbling *Hot Mess* on the spackled wall
in the spaces between where my fucks had painted their names
and/or identifiers, i.e., *The Red Carousel*, in my bedroom
where the morning lights never quite reached me
but sometimes hovered. After I would drop a glass
or lose my balance, the angels would carry me into my room
& place me in my cot then leave, locking the door behind them.
I would lay awake for hours listening to them debate
about my heaven, argue over the true meanings behind
my infantile poems, & groan over my choice of women & men.
I would listen to them pray to the creator or the created or the faceless
Goddess I had yet to meet; pray on my behalf for my salvation.
For a year, it was as if I was both alive & dying.
The most beloved of the city's urchins—the most possessed
by nature & spirit.

Photo of a Girl, 1993: Bitch

Fort Hood, Texas

a pack of eighteen-wheelers out hunting along the rain-soaked highways
suffocate the word before it reaches into my second-floor window.

below, our neighbor's eyes /click/click/ open,
his brows arched up as he stares over the gate & into our backyard.

i ~~flinch when his flat pink lips slide~~ open & reveal
~~charred gums & piss~~ teeth. ~~when my dog begins to~~ howl & buck.

daddy brings the stud up behind her again—cups her hips & holds
her still when the cock catches her off guard. her fur dampens,

the muscle jerking beneath, but he holds her still until the stud jars her open
& our neighbor's cheeks gash red & suck. i watch the neighbor & not her & he is

clearly shaken. panting a little, he parts his lips—hunting for a name. a tool
both my father & this man can share while watching her get taken.

& it is in their eyes—at the way that she is
finally broken into.

Dog Catchers in Texas

How I catch them in the Southwest: With sweet butter & sangria. *Wild waters in strange places.* With a shovel full of coral snakes. *With names & missing fathers.* Con horchatas. Con handmade flour tortillas. *Con mis caderas.* With spare guitar strings, bare feet, & thin house dresses. *With porches. With poorly whittled totems.* With blessed stones & the echo of the hills. *With the always stretch of hungry land.*

All the beer & corn they can stand. I catch them

with their own hope, stiff in their empty pockets. With the promise: *You too can lose ghosts in these striations.* Or else find them in these hills. *Either way, get lost.* Boys come in from all over. *In every shade of sand.* Pretty peach boys & vanilla bean boys. Men in full blue-black & sunteased browns.

Los Gallos del Desierto. Once.

I'd arch over to meet them. Bend the tanned rear till it was a super moon. Till the belly swayed under it. *A hammock crest beneath this body.* My mud-bruised thighs would rub themselves cayenne, slap out a hymn. *Spread like cut roasted peppers.* Broil under a sauced San Marcos afternoon.

Boys would rut & rut & linger, long after. *Still panting.* Drool weeping down penny-colored covered skin. I'd obey. *Roll over.* Pretend.

They would pay me for this.
I would let them.

wanted.

You rode me—
my body being made
for this sort of thing—
like I was your Mother,
exhaust of precipice;
grunting *I cannot*
remember Her.
Rocks popped under foot,
summer foamed
against my tit, swelled
against the bark
as you rode
my crescent split
all up & all weapon
in your hands.
Tequila eclipsed
your meat-hugged mouth
& slipped down my hips
now more round
with the authority
of these years
después de tequila.
Do you remember now?
Hours came & left
& I was bent over
the plunged bole
of some acrid tree
in the middle of a road
somewhere, on the island
of your Mother's father
with your fat risk
begging
inside of me.

It would become
a deep bruise—
familiar & missed—
like the warmth
of my years-dead husband
or the love
of our apparatus Mothers.
Where is your father? I asked.
Probably in the wrong tense.
Where are your people?
You said
nothing.
Aimed me down
& crowned me
in the bush.
Dug your heels
into the dirt
& sank.

Hex for R. Kelly

i

Dress the black candle in vinegar, write his name in needle.
Pay Death his fifteen cents & place your hands on the table in prayer.

ii

Wind from the South:

provoke the incense in his name,
stagger flicks of light like daggers
through the man & all he claims,
asses to ashes, incinerate the fame.

Wind from the North:

crawl like static in his blood,
remove the tempo & its chains,
fold his body in your glove,
compress the movement in his frame.

Wind from the West:

steal the breath from out his lungs,
trap all the air in his belly,
snatch the follicle before it's sprung,
scatter the shed skin & demolish all his bones.

Wind from the East:

let down your splendid veil,
turn away your shining face,

leave him to his hell.
may his seed dry up.

May his weapon never again swell.

Featuring Tonight at the Street-Hustler's Circus: The Girls

The streets ram themselves into coochies:
sodden women with bamboo for backs
& taffy for sex. *Both sweet & sour.*

Star-cloaked women who don't bend
or break. Who catch Hondas right in they grills.
Women with electric-pink hoofs that drag

in the slow churn of the intersection. Clog
the sidewalks. Metastasize along the corridor
of Main Street. They have come to settle

around the bend of this corner. Pose
under carnival-like car lights at just nine-thirty.
Note: *It ain't even prime time & they got all that*

good-good going on sale. The gully accordion,
their arms sway in & out of tempo with traffic.
They stagger in & out of the busted frame of Pop's

Grocery neon-blue *OPEN* sign. Their smoke-thin throats
glitter when they slip into the ring center of the hotel lobby.
Strangled light bubbles & soaps along their jaws like melted crayons

through the Plexiglas. A rush of shade strains
against their nylon-clamped thighs, rides up their hips
& dangles around their soft bellies as they saunter on in.

They be harvested sounds for the replay later this evening.
When they got to make it do what it do. When they got to
cash they own checks. Trace dollar signs into ceilings—signals

cut with their zirconia encrusted toes.
Giggle & grunt at all the right moments
for the *Best in Show.*

The Daughters of Samuel Little

left unburied to rot, black girls
writhe on asphalt. their shadows seethe
& seek out their ancestors. call on papa
legba in search of roots. seek a denouement
for black girls. call on all living & lived
& lost. but black girls blend into
backwoods. slip into soil. feed crops.
all unburied. cut in. out. shimmer
in back-road ditches. fauna lost.
seek a truth to their sentence & exile.
hovering. the night opera. never enough
of a problem here. gorged sewers cough.
exile now sounds sovereign. like it's a gift.
a little air. black girls abandon this town. a blessing.
absent the gris-gris. absent the wool cut. trickle
back into rusted pipelines. blood in the water.
moan. sputter. cling to hands bleached clean.
they know that there is never enough evidence.
become a curse on the head of this city. become
the aching in this asphalt for: something.

Photo of a Girl, 1995: Training Day
Somewhere, Texas

Per my Mother's instructions:
my sisters & I have sewn

our palms into our hips,
clipped our necks 45 degrees;

are shadows leaning side by side;
DANGER

with our fat grins & fanny packs.
We are—all of us—carrying

switchblades in our panties now.
Momma says *If you have to*

walk home alone tonight, act
like you crazy. Talk to yourself—

they won't want you then.
So we master the art of aggression.

We mumble in our sleep, mumble in
our own snapchat filter–laden language;

gussy up with our acrylic claws
& ochre painted chains;

grow legs that reach out
in every direction—thick-hipped spiders

crawling down metallic runways
& up holly-stained carpets,

strutting across busy highways,
lying flat under houses washed in snow.

We learn to step hard
through pop-up galleries;

flex in the second skins of our gowns;
shed our pelts for our prescriptions;

swivel/click/pop/swivel/click/pop
rotate on our pedestals

for the paying pedestrians;
crow at the bystanders,

bark at the hooded
eyes of strangers, & at some

point, it is no longer acting.
We are asking ourselves

very important questions: *Is this my home?*
Are you my father? Are these your children?

How much will you give me for them?
How much? Are these your glasses?

How much? It's twenty for a blow job,
ten for my foot up your ass.

What about my ass? What about
my ass? Is this your degree?

Are you a doctor? Can you help me with this?
With this right here? Can you help me?

Are you down with OPP? Can you feel me?
Motherfucker—can you feel me?

For years, I stare into my sister's mirror
& try to remember my name

but my Mother has matched us all
in fade-to-black jeans & ghost tees;

we are—all of us—identical
fractures in the concrete

& I am no longer the woman
I would have been.

We are—all of us—prepared
for the apocalypse,

for the inevitability of chaos.
We are—all of us—a war

of our own now, a panic etched
into the soft metals of our backs,

lining the hollow barrels of our legs.
We are—all of us—shades of kerosene.

Armed. Aimed. Ready.
I am—now—a weapon

prepared to distract & destroy
your comfort for my survival.

It is now—second nature—to unveil
& persevere in this body.

The program has been fully installed
& I am unable to follow commands

from unknown servers.
[Esc+Esc]

I am the shrapnel
littering your streets;

I am the vessel
living next door;

I am the sniper drinking wine
in your living room;

the missile seeking comfort
in your bed.

Concrete Qweens

We grazed like deer on the cold
corner of Fifth & Trinity. Posted up
with our contoured cheeks & our matte lips
& our "Yas, girl! Remy waves on swim!"
With our stacked bodies—stacks on stacks
on stacks—our swollen chests, our slim waists,
our juicy hips on slay. No one knew the better.
We huddled together & prayed to a god who
hummed blue & green for anything good.
A god who sings & sings forever in our ears
& never sleeps & knows all things. In line,
we stood on the corner, whistled
when the light clicked green—
then red then green—
without us ever moving. Us,
with the giraffe necks & the ashy ankles
rooted in filthy concrete, leaning
every now & then into traffic.
We bit through the rust & paint
of the STOP sign. Chewed through
the hours of our youth. Glared
into the smoking sun.
Some of us wondering about
what we didn't know about.
It was why we stood out
in the middle of the street—waiting
for the screech & halt, the sudden crush
of a city college like a fist full of dollars,
to ride on up against our broad backs & clipped hips.
We just wanted to know. We were all-knowing
yet still without a thought that mattered enough
to save us from ourselves
or the *CLAPCLAP* of gats gone pedestrian.

Posted up on the corner of Fifth & Trinity
without a confession or anything holy
to keep us innocent, we got bored. *Shit!*
We hit the lobbies. Hit up the other corners
(previously occupied by our mothers
but now by our fine asses). *Shit!*
We got to posting up our pictures
in the WANTED section,
with our gummy tummies & thighs
all primed & ready. How were they gonna know
what we wanted if we didn't tell them?
How were we supposed to catch our break
if we didn't bend? We good for constellations
like that. Pull from ourselves the shine & pivot
for prestige. Make for ourselves a way through
the poorly lit theaters of the world. I mean, just last night
World Star came to film us. They heard
we would do anything; wanted to
know which one of us would
twerk for a scholarship.
The girls: *You don't got to*
ask me twice! We were all creative
entrepreneurs—except for Zaire.
Zaire had to leave, had to go pick up her son.
Said she'd be back later. And this other girl
whose name I can't remember
called her daughter over & they did this whole routine.
Like they just knew. They had their own
theme song & everything. They got a whole extra stack
to do the *Swalla*. Momma on one end, daughter on the other.
They gobbled & gobbled till their lips touched
& everyone laughed & hollered. It was fun—
but I knew that I had to go.

I couldn't stay. I grabbed my books
& told them *I already got mine.*
This was just pocket money. Girl, bye.
And the rest lined up against the wall
& arched their backs.
I was in a hurry—
but I think we all know
what happened after that.

Tinder

the blonde Uber driver
with my address, name & number

the bear-faced bohemian barista
with my name & number

the slickly coiffed bachelor posing on the bar
waiting for my number

the "distinguished" professor dangling
a network of names & numbers

the educated brotha from Howard U.
crossing the sands & drippin' numbers

the fox of a boy dragging denim skins
around his ankles, hollerin' "Gimme dat numba!"

the father | father | father | father | daddy—
just outta lockup today—with my number

the "woke" sis with the detachable dick
who straight-up took my number

the Christ-whipped child of heaven
who straight-up took my number

the crooning coward: a hooded siren
tearing into the soft beginnings of names & numbers—

may you ocean of fleas,
finally, be dusted

with a lifetime
of reckonings

Photo of a Girl, 1996: Conjurer

Killeen, Texas

daddy says *milk bone*　　　clinches the cartilage

of my name between his grated palms　　　& my Momma's

souped tongue　　　Momma says *you nasty cow*

& i shit milk.　　　curdle in my panties.

cross my legs　　　at the dinner table　　　to hush my bell

heavy-belly　　　& it takes years

for me to learn　　　how to open my mouth　　　wide enough to say

move

but when i finally do　　　my sisters torque into　　　fat bronze bowls

brimming with white　　　silk & salt　　　their loaded bodies

dripping ceaselessly

with the holler

of

woman

Photo of X, 2005: What Dreams Are These?

Somewhere, Somewhere

Again, I am dreaming of a promise:
one I made when I was too young to know
the consequence of such a thing.

Again, I am dreaming of mountains
doused in burning indigos. My body—
anchored to the skyline—is a fog
that bleeds for days. Like the stretch of land
that rubs against every city, the road
tethers itself to my wrist & drags me back
h/o/m/e: outlined in chalk—a festering thing
like the hoods in which I was never a child.
Fort Hood. Compton. Baltimore. Chicago.
My point is—I was never a child; always
a movement.

>As I drive from the white river of San Marcos
>to the roux-scented woods of New Orleans—
>at the beckoning of an ancestor I have yet to name—
>acres of otherwheres vault at my presence,
>their tiny green hairs urgent & stiff
>along their feral backs.

>Headlights flash like two suns dying
>every evening & waking ivy on the walls of my eyelids
>to crawl up against the borders
>of this house & climb inside.

>The highway, basted with brick dust, swirls
>like whiskey at my feet,
>the hills running out before me,
>their spines bent & tummies slack
>below the dirt.

Again, I am dreaming of a dollar-hungry hand
punishing an elevator door; my twitching ass
bent forward at the front of a congested welfare line.
I remember who I was twenty-four hours before
I sniffed a cloud from atop the sticky glass
of his coffee table; evacuated my body to find
my body a sticky portal through which gods came;
my body a doorway for erect figures
& their gaudy excess; when I was not dripping
in remnant; when I was a woman & not
a memory.

*Beforebeforebeforebeforebeforebeforebeforebeforebeforebeforebeforebefore
beforebeforebeforebeforebeforebeforebeforebeforebeforebeforebeforebefore
beforebeforebeforebeforebeforebeforebeforebeforebeforebeforebeforebefore*
I was a fist of a second mouth *beforebeforebefore* I was a place where men came
    to die *beforebeforebeforebeforebeforebeforebeforebeforebefore* I mastered
       the art of suffocation *beforebeforebefore* I watched myself be eaten
          beforebeforebeforebeforebeforebefore
        I was an assassin of doubt & circumstance
        beforebeforebeforebeforebeforebefore
      I was a wife *before* I was a wife *before* I was a girl
        who dreamed a husband. *Before* I was a girl
         who had real faith in the good of men;
          when I trusted their iron & justified scales.

                If I had a wooden nickel
             for every dozen, I'd be retired.
            But I ain't. So give me a hand!
              My hand, My hands
          have learned to clap hymns & sing
           for themselves. My hands beat

themselves into dragon-washed floors,
into tables cloaked in candles & little black boys
who've turned
into fiends. Little brown boys
who have learned to pop locks
& rummage—maggots—
after the fact. They come,
angry & hot: in my little black box.
seething. Always
looking for my money.

Again, I am dreaming of a body
I left:

In Taos. In Indiana.
In Columbus. In Detroit.
In Chicago. In DC. In Atlanta.
In Jersey. In Philly.
In Boston. In Fort Worth. In Austin

bodies are stacked like twenties on my dresser,
next to the cologne & cognac. *I win! I win!*
I told them to never gamble with an insomniac.
After 3:00 a.m. anything makes dollars & sense.

I remade myself out of smoke & iron,
rubbed myself down in gasoline, & came
over to they house.

Herald all you morticians
scraping the noise of my moan
off of their corpses!
Keep the residue of

my residuals for yourself.
Taste it! Put it in your mouth!
Sweet, isn't it? See?
I gave more than I got
& I only took what was given.
And I am again, hungry!
Warn the others! I am coming!
Don't be mad I found a way
to get my body back. Don't be mad
that I went & got what was coming to me.
It was coming for me. Don't be mad
you can't take what I got.

Don't be mad!
Hey!
Don't be mad!

I mean, if you didn't want me here,
you should've turned out the streetlights.

Again, I am dreaming of a sunrise.
One whose grit & grime–covered ass
got me all hot & bothered. I couldn't help but snatch
off the ropes around my legs & split wide for her.
Get her on my side. *Good morning!* My mouth
between her sunrays, she kept screaming
I am dreaming of a prayer! Of a prayer! Of a prayer!
& I just had to shut her up—so I fell into her
here in Texas. Dug a bowl into her belly & drank.

Again, I am dreaming of a boy
& I dream of his womb. I dream of needles
in his spine. I dream of god threading my kiss

there. Marrying my arms around his neck,
collapsing my legs around his hips. I dream
forever after this. Bore of such dreaming,
dream instead of tomorrow & next week & next year.

                              There is a country: an allotted land
                                with a bed for me in it. A place
                                where I will—finally—sleep.
                                 And this land—let it keep
                              only this body. Let it keep only this—
                               this room with too many windows.

Collage of a Dying Sun

He is dying to hear the echo
of his rubber wheels running down
the arched back of an empty garage parking lot,
to climb the fat trunks of trees
crowding the street he grew up on,
to get married in his backyard
beneath a mar of eager & fresh roses—
so we elope. Only to find our marriage
is a rupture of sound & method.
We fuck the whole afternoon,
coaxing stars from the attics of our mouths;
removing our clothes, those costume carcasses,
to charter the atlas of ourselves.
I press my body against his
nakedness, lean over the edge
of his shoulder to listen to:
the whip & crack
of a constant sun unfurling
in his chest; the slow burn
of it all like the tetras of a lost moon
tearing into the tendons that swim
in the bend of him; the diptych aurora
of our gravities hushing themselves
in the palpable heat
swindled between our knees;
his inevitable confession: *I am dying.*
He is dying to watch the moon collapse
into a cobalt lining—so quietly
we listen to the wolves
commanding the desert in the dark
& he kisses the scars on my ashy legs;
swallows whole liters of absinthe,
becomes gravity sans kinetic.

The next morning, we ride silent,
listen to songs about soldiers & wars
he will never know, pass orchid shades
asleep on the bodies of the mountains
we avoid & refuse to see. Roads
change colors & fade into trees
along crooked lines
in the arid & empty hills.
Suddenly, it's as if all the confessions
of our climax, once allowed to atrophy,
expand. This is when he loves me enough
to say: *I want a little girl.*
So we pull over to make one,
hold each other up
until electric sapphire leaks
in through the fogged-up motel windows.
Until our chrysalis, softly wet, lies open
on the carpet beside the mirror.
That night he tries to fly
from ten flights up
& I make him promise
to never leave the bed again.
But he murmurs *But I am tired*
& lilac stains the chalky walls
of that white room while we hum,
our mouths chasing an absence.
We laugh, we sigh, & soon I am saying
I think this urn is far too small to hold him.

The Red Wedding Dress

Had I known my waist would become a trip wire
of baby girls, before/then a bed of broken shells

beneath tainted lace, I would not have chosen
—from across the room—the dress that screamed

Love me, dear & hummed a furnace against my breast
just like his mouth at the breakfast table:

a bonfire that danced on the lips of my skirt,
an omen of the eggs that would fall.

But it did scream & so: in the dress shop
I twirled & twirled—winter's stag

silhouetted before a dying sun
—a hot ache against all the beige.

My bleeding threads muscling through
the bland husks of a million naïve brides.

My Sister-Wife

I share my husband
with his grave.
She chews on
the strange stillness
of his quiet unravel;
an undoing—
like thread—
slow & always.
Same as when
he first moved
inside of me
as an escape
of air, an exhale
scrawled between
the bridge
of our salt.
Where he sleeps,
the ground sweats
against my foot, familiar
with the work
of reconstruction.
All things come to
& from. Knowing
this, I dig
into his brother.
I chew. Suck in salt.
Crack my jaw. Open
& spit out the shell.
Nothing is safe.
What is sacred?
I wonder where
the water went,
lay my palm

against my bone,
berate the mangled hair,
paddle along
my heavier thighs, whine
with my hips rusted over
& unattended to,
weep for where
I felt him fill me last.
Out of necessity,
each night turns
out like this.
Out of pity,
I let Her
savor the rank
of him.

Lazarus

my mouth empties itself into long stretches of nowhere
your name in suspension   still lives where the grasses hiss
any lick of land alongside hwy 70

sometimes i drive in the dark for hours   until i can feel you hovering
like a bowl of light   stratifying dozens of doped supermoons
through the slip of my tinted windshield

magnetic   how the hours rope around my wrist now
a constant ring around me   it is you extending eternally
& i miss you like lost luggage

the water over travis lake sifts   & i hear you moan beneath it
i climb the trunk of tallest acacia i can find
& listen to you vibrate in the hollow   i. have. tried.

my love, i have tried to fill the empty archive of these arms
but   but   but   it was you
forever   cavernous & often   grief holds me still

& your name is a litanylitanylitany   of porcelain prayers
scattered between the years after you fell into permanence
& after i put myself back together

i have cross-dialed the plains for you   in search of hills for pasture
a place where i could perch on the highest rock facing east   jump into after-sun
it feels as though   i have already lived

too many times for this sort of dream—with all of its glamorous eternity
you have made a martyr of me   siphoned whatever was left innocent
left me a triggerless barrel   barren

if it brought me to you   i would split this self
between sacred & the altar of
lazarus   i ache for you   in the parts of me that still yield

About My Daughter Who I Gave A Way

She will roam
until she finally knows
what it is to begin to end—
an echo still hot
on the broken floors
of a cave in Taos;
a squealing wheel
on the back half
of the last train
from uptown Chicago;
an untamed stallion
from the red dirts
of Oklahoma; crested
by a thousand nights
of wondering—
the question
will ride her.
I will explain:
I whittle sound
for a living,
hatchet suns
in the back of a parlor,
interpret chaos
for quarters & free coffee.
I will warn her
about happiness—
lesson her
on the making of
& suggest
the ways
in which to avoid it.

The Third Rite of Smoke

Li'l Mama Gets High

remembers she got a degree in "bitch. please." minored in proper english but these white folks still don't know what the fuck she mean when she say: us restless daughters forage under neon lights for leftover liquor & boy-meat, never pretending perfection, we discuss the cons of your heaven, climb concert speakers & swallow full moons. petition deejays with our chocolate-filled hips. make it rain on them. grind the earth & give you gardens. rub our legs together & give you smoke. suck hoodoo down our parched muscle. cough up glitter & gore. *sometimes for your amusement but never for your approval.* us restless daughters have waned on the idea of separation from our spiritual selves. are no longer your cannibals. are no longer your christians. have gotten into grand discussions about no longer covering up our baartman bodies. have learned to covet our scars. learned to worship the skin we survive in. question the purpose of religion *& other nonsense shit like that.* believe in the spirit: *the measurable force—like light—pushing & pulling between here & whatever comes after.* us restless daughters believe in [   ]. curate its space in our homes. seek out our equals. get lit up—talking about transitions & transformations. get lit up— talking about the scientific evidence of good vibes. get lit up—*& that's the problem.* we are still wondering how we always manage to end up alone *& face down in a pool of gasoline.* we have got to love ourselves out here. us restless daughters stone the silence—our black bodies hang from the stars *like hot oil under blemished sun.* shimmy when everyone else is asleep. *dig into ourselves.* dig under—blocks & blocks of black bodies—for fresh water. under the side streets. groan for our broken pipes. *our stolen gardens.* look for where it all went wrong. dig the ruined parts out. reach inside ourselves because somebody—*somebody*—has got to fix the goddamned plumbing in here.

A Tale from the Hood

Undercover, the triggers
of chalk-dusted goons tripped
on the local game of niggas
they was hunting. Caught
everybody off guard.
And these fools thought
it was all just gonna go away.
They canceled the TV crews
& the coroners & the internal
investigations. Told everyone:
Just go home. It's over. But it
wasn't over. It's never over. It
got the traumatized & taunted—
aunties/mamas/grandmamas—
to congress over they forgotten
& call down they ancestors.
Summon up the rooted. Go live.
And boo: They. was. not. ready.

Moon-eaters swarm & hum
under the fluorescent trick
of the busted streetlight
over on Fifth. Swell & flood out
the alley. All of them, hooded
spooks on howl. Apparitions
of chopped tar-dipped diamonds
grinning cement teeth. Their faces
beat jigsaw, their bodies slick
as graffiti—they've come back
to get what they're owed.

B b L l A a C c K k acid bleeding
all over the streets, they drippin'
coagulated cayenne like they is
those girls. Just girls before
the nick & chomp; before the city caught
they bodies; before the city slipped into
they bodies, but now—they flares
of mauve light, rockin' inflamed chests
& split cherry tongues; they swollen throats
full of fire. They eyes on hot
like ruptured dwarf stars.

Before they were graffiti,
they were boys. Before steel hymns
whispered holes into them,
they were boys. Just boys
before the chop & flip;
before they were separated
bone from rib; before the city
got under they skin for good,
they was boys—but now, they jugs
full of lightning—swirling summer
storms in their smoke-infused cheeks,
pushing havoc up through they filtered lungs
& out through they Gucci pursed lips.

They air colliding with scripture
like Molotov cocktails & brick walls.

Kaleidoscope Cracked Wide Open
on Fifth and Trinity

it is a bad day to be
a ghost. a wanderer.
ghosts too—can bleed,
i have discovered.

an exorcism in my cul-de-sac
is the exodus
of the only other black boy
i know who lives
here. now
my iris is
more broken glass
than epic hydrant,
is accompanied
by a symphony
of groaning women
who flood the block,
their hands
perpetually
reachingreaching
for the bodies
of their excavated sons.
i watch
the priest, navy skinned & afraid
wrestle back his steel rosary,
trying to calm
the snapping jaw
of a devastated genesis—
a woman, invoking
fire & brimstone.
he fails to quiet
her insanity & i feel

carmine torches flare
up from the cavity of her
lips. i feel
myself flower in her
sudden expulsion
& we become
a battering ram of melanin,
punishing the yellow rope
around the neck of our child;
a simulacrum
of blanched hues
growing heavy
with night.

i feel Her breed
Her anger with our smoke
& become:

The Guillotine
from Crenshaw,

The Hook
of the South.

The Mother
in us all

—lit.

Photo of X, 2010: A Box of Wine

San Marcos, Texas

Where my head hit the floor—there is a pool
of pink light. Spillages where I drowned
last night in my kitchen. There are seven years' worth
of blood moons in my kitchen, stuffed into plastic
bags & cardboard boxes. There are stains
deep-set down down down my occipital
& they are down all over the kitchen
covering the alabaster bodies:
of the counter, the table, the defunct
dishwasher—marking the where
of every attack I've ever made against the grind
of my gentle suffocations & patient drownings.
I count how many times I've slipped
into something less comfortable. Less familiar.
How many times was I a pillar of salt?
How many times was I
a weapon? How many times was I
an inflamed shade against the light? A tacky flush
blotting the linoleum?
A pregnant ampersand? My kitchen is wet
with seven years' worth of mournings & laughter.
Yolked mornings & meaty-scented nights.

sandboxes.

I smile
at all the babies
I see. Secret them
rows of bleached teeth.
Flinch when mothers
bury them into boxes
slick with bird bones
& cat piss & broken glass;
when rose blooms on smudged cheeks—
hot with other infections—
& I wonder if this is common
practice.
do they know
what is down there?
do they care
about what is down there?
what is down there?
do mothers care about
there? *down there?*
do other mothers care
about what is down there?
do other mothers care
about other mothers?
do other mothers bury
their children there,
on purpose? *down there?*
do other mothers whisper
to their children there?
down there? do other mothers
whisper to their phantom children?
do other mothers see their children
in other arms? do other mothers
try to forget what date it is?

what date is it now? is it that day?
do other mothers know it is that day?
do they care? do other mothers care
it is that day? do they stop to pray
in between orgasms, these other mothers?
do they still orgasm, these other mothers?
can other mothers orgasm after there?
down there? do other amputee mothers
congregate outside of other homes?
other theres? other anywheres?
do other mothers scream
into empty bassinets & empty car seats
in back seats & empty bedrooms
down empty hallways? *do they always?*
do they scream always? do they crochet
their blankets to smother their theres?
their down theres? *do they smother*
their down theres? do other mothers sob
at the spasms of their empty bellies?
do their bellies spasm? do they still feel
it down there? do they mourn their thefts?
do they mourn? do other mothers mourn?

When She Young, Black, & Bad

I love this city for its weeping,
how the city grieves
when it finally remembers me;
how it follows me for a block,
then jogs up the stairs after me
with an eye for my pelt—
I've never felt so wanted;
how at the site of my toothy grin
it clinches its leather bag
against its tight & sinew
as though it is trying to pull me in
onto the El where the people agitate
themselves into pint boxes
like cattle—graze on the parched faces
of the lonely & the underpaid
traveling up from down South—
it knows that I am always hungry;
how the people of this city hurry past
the paralyzed children to get to the colorless
widows who still grieve out in public
with their hands smelling like takeout
& pussy & me; how the people of this city
aggravate the traffic with their bodies,
throw themselves into intersections
in front of bent yellow-bellied hoods—
just trying to get closer to me;
I love that they march head on
into heavy here; that they do not fear
their own death. They fear this Shine.

Saint She of All the Missing Things

I let the crazy have me
& now I mourn in technicolor—

jiggle when I sob; a manifest of loss
& broken vows. I haven't stopped

saying your name since they set you
on fire. Dear Viking: You ride me

in my sleep & I float to razed shores.
It is as expected: our love was transitory, full

of regress & fatal attractions; things came
to die, or end, or part here. Each night

is a casket of rain; every morning is a tidal wave;
the afternoon, a soaked sheet of a marriageless bed;

every evening—thick with jackals that dig
up my dead. The days are asylums, the nights

are nurses with turned backs; the hours—
just walls that lecture me, windows that quiver

against my lips. The doctors avert their eyes now
& call their mentors about my root. My teeth

are obsidian blades, my jaw is never dull;
my tongue like the dagger of christ

culling the light from poor men's veins.
Dear Almost-Husband: you have made a wife

out of minced meat: me, swallowing shreds
of myself, daily.

Photo of X, 2011: The Suicide Disease

Chicago, Illinois

It happens. My mouth is cut, the sliced lid of an envelope.
A perfectly split, notoriously wide, opulent blood orange.

If you peer down the hatch, you find a sort of telescope;
a sort of rip in the occipital range, cauterized & singed.

The wretched vein flicks, pops at light, bows even to an eyelash.
It satchels itself to the bridge of my brow: a thinning wire,

a poor man's critique of mortality, a standard-issue mustache.
It groans under the skin, humbles itself, brushes as swallowed fire.

The body is a burial ground, a reversed birth, a chaos underhand.
Is an overflow of traumatic stretch, the pain is ripe for render.

I never see it coming. The static pause, the ampersand.
I can never catch its tail, the slough of skin made tender.

How the wound spills, acrylic map along the temple, precise & photogenic;
the breed of after-light personified, I tether pomegranate.

murder.

there are those never discovered under this short sky's trap of wind &
water. never caught. found. their screams clotted by city halls. hundreds
of bricks between the missing & found. never exonerated for their other-
whereness. their exhales gravel-stuffed into sternums. buried beneath
blocks of mud. the ash-heavy grass of a parish lawn. i am old enough to
know the difference between the dead & the living. to know the difference
between *fresh* & *demolition*. old enough to recognize when death is safe in
this city. harbored. hidden away beneath. hushed. there are those disguised
by the monotony of train tracks. stowed away in shadows. wrapped in large
plastic bags. coppered sand. positioned upright as though they only fell
asleep. forgot to awake the next day. evidence themselves. remnant bully. in
the gully. underneath their nails. there are those left buried in pits. under
parking lots. in alleyway crevices. beside dumpsters tagged neon green &
ghoul. there are those who hang from dozens of windowsills like strange
tomatoes. heavy with routine. the beat. blue. black. *mostly black* routine.
blue. beat with decades of suns. missing faces. bloated. angry. all of them
sweaty & beautiful & trifling. all of them. empty after morning. heavy. in
plain sight.

Graffiti: An American Sonnet for Eric Garner

slang for *amen,* a man hisses I AM in electric blue.
cherry spits THEY CAN'T ARREST US ALL over blue-black top.

slang for *fuck the police*: something knocked loose in us hisses nonstop.
drips & sustains like electric sunsets: hot acrylic DNA from the crew.

slang for *contemporary art*: it interprets blank spaces, city-wide canvases in queue;
the walls are alive & well & full of seen things; here a man. there his daughter. popped.

slang for *this my house*: it is the root word *graphein*: is a graft placed over the clocked.
vigilante crayons flicker quick-wrist sutures into stucco, tryna dial in healing hues.

greek for *I've got something to say*: it is now on the cover of *Time.*
juxtaposed with blasted rooftops & cars crowned with fire, is a sign, is now evidence.

is now chalk vandals with gallery salaries, brown digits with cuffs & tickets.
slang for *god's gray hair*: in hi-res it highlights all crossed lines.

the language of *gawd*: *& she is* not used to being told what & where & how to do it,
                                is now just a pretty blue sky covered in rainbow shit.

Letter to Black Girls

Dangle god over water. Don't listen to his pleas & cock
your head to the side to see him turn red in the face. If he is
white, watch his pockets empty themselves
of rocks made of scripture, praise made of copper.

Remember that joy is a horse in the dirt,
without a rein or a rider. Let zeal crawl deep
in the muscle of your face, scurry down your legs,
grow calluses on the bottoms of your feet.

Don't forget. The spirit is a distillery of virtue
& fiction. Nothing is ever as true as death
or the newfound orgasm; the long-awaited yawn
of the universe—finally forgiving
the body in which it was bred,
with waves of dark light & star dust.

Year of the Dog

On an evening as golden & cold as this,
there came a clarity as thick & refined
as any hill on the acre. Justice. It is

> as out of reach for the at-risk & the homeless,
> as out of reach for the uneducated & the blue collared,
> as out of reach for the full bellied & the right-handed,
> as out of reach for the surefooted & the brilliant,
> as out of reach for the promised & the refused
> all still dark with the desert & Congo.

As it is for all dogs & other foul creatures.
As it has always been for me—since before I learned to run.

ii

We whine when one gets loose
& jumps over the fence, ending up
on a sidewalk too far downtown.

We pace & shit on piles of old newspapers,
with fake news in the headlines, white faces
covering black bodies up with they bylines.

We sniff the strange meat we find
strewn across our front yard, overturned
in the backyard, poked through in the cul-de-sac.

We question the brown edges like *Who threw this shit
down in front of my house?* Start wondering
Where the damn babies at anyways?

iii

How do you hang a dog with his own neck?
Throw him into the back of a van.

How do you crack a dog's spine without cracking a smile?
Chain that dog up to air & throw him into the back of a van.

How do you make sure man's best friend never becomes a man?
Give him his collar back, reattach the leash, and throw that dog—
  back into the van.

iv

Do ya chains hang low?
Do they wobble? Is they gold?

If they ain't, can I go?
Can I go? Can I go?

v

My throat raw with all that barking
at the smoke in the streets. Mad
'cause I been conjured—coaxed
to sob & howl.

Even with all that root work
down in the bloody house of Gawd—
we've all got funeral wreaths
for necks now.

vi

Now we all gonna get out the gate.
Catch a body. Get these bodies back.

Pick up the dead & howl & *Shit*.
As far as I'm concerned:

anything & everything
can burn!

The Kids Are Gonna Be Alright

Ratchet tongues slurp on cool shades at after-school kickbacks,
suck on trap music rolling tide through the cracked glass
of Lil' Trunk's mama's busted-ass Dodge. Clouds of sound
POP from the fourth floor of the complex behind them
& everyone looks for a trigger. Hot-oiled scalps
swish back black box braids against the skyline
& hiss laughter into the breached mouth of summer.
They push back against the clock-ins & hustles & histories
they know like the smalls of they backs. They know it's time
to glow up & trade in bathroom passes for bus passes,
ride from South Side to *outta here.* They gone
learn the jig like they learned all the other jigs:
It ain't never been that hard. Backpacks & money bags
have always been the same for them: hungry.
They ain't got time for stress. Red-bones slip up steps to break
bread with ox kings & onyx queens, who dip then roll
to bops in mock cyclones—parking-lot pot winners
& everyone everywhere is hands in the air—
you know they gonna push & pull it together.
Just like they learned to.

For the White Girl in Poetry Workshop Who Says
I Don't Belong Here

i cut out all the parts you wouldn't like about this. decided to leave only:

the femur.
the fibula.
the thorax.
        my neck, swiveling skull
        a clicking vertebra, the spine
        or the tail. *what is left of it anyways.*

my knees—still bleeding—fresh.
for you, my sweet.

        the jaw grind. my ground teeth.
        chatter. chatter. chit. chit.
        i sleep with too many words in my mouth.
mouth, in

        the catcher.
        the dream—catcher—in my chest.

the left shoe. the wrong foot.

        the note: *read for further instructions.*
        a single tube of bitch. *the lipstick, my dear.*
        my ruptured lung. the slinky.

i put a spell in this. *for you, my dear.*

a pastor. green. a pen like a pink tooth.
i wish you ink that bleeds.
a well. blxck & fat. a hungry thing.

the hand.
       the Saturn.
       the binary four.
       the digitus medius.

for you, my sweet.

Black Escapism

When we finally begin to break,
our bones shattering under the serrated tongue

of a scalpel in our beloved brother's hands,
after having known our father's steel motive,

weighted ardently upon the strident chords
cocooned in our flightless bodies,

in accordance with the wool laughter
stretched too thinly across our mother's chin,

agile as the buffed legs of any loose muse liquored—
we itch to taste the sweet vinegar graze of Joy,

a finite whiskey hurried down our throats.
A deterrent of sorts, roaring gloriously in our gut,

bubbling against our lips as laughter. Joy—
a final offense against the defiling of hours;

a final defense against the sluggish corrosion
of our pitiful outfits; a final relief

to the sore skins we became too accustomed to.
To be black and a woman is to be full of rage—

the ligament of hope and grief—to be
constructed from the best of the wreck

but unable to sustain our buoyant bodies
in the terrible sea of our years.

To be black and a woman is to sift
through the waves, in search of purpose.

Before we are forced to surrender to one
of our many kinds of death, we will let Joy

sear every inch where breath once belonged,
until pain is phantom and we stand no more.

All It Took to Get to You

The chances are slim that I should come to you—
& I gutted my way through hell to get here

blood begets blood   *salt-running earth*   as do the gates of women

unpacked unceremoniously   *my body, a cannon*   in sterilized rooms

hospitals beget wombs   *my child, a stone*   cracked open in unison:

two hundred & fifty-five rips   *a pillar of salt*   every minute

begets five point two   *suffocated potentials*   murderers/lovers

every one-thousand souls   *we were the same once*   anchors survived

every black body   *daughters to gorges*   survived

begets the chances that   *my child, a weapon*   we—even make it

to this moment   *we were the same once*   we found love

or became something more   *both daughters to machines*   we made it out

alive *& we gutted our way through hell to get here*
                    & into each other's arms

Photo of X, 2007: HoodWitches
Somewhere, Somewhere

#hallelujah to the HoodWitches
to the shellac clapbacks & neck-roll snaps
of sistahs who snatch tracks & dodge ditches.
#blessedbe to they too small kitchens.
#blessedbe they dolla-tree gumbo.
#blessedbe they cokes & hot cheetos.
may the gawds smile down
& rain money on some of us bxtches.
#imdifferent
descended from the truth-eaters,
i swallowed sarah saartjie baartman.
she buried herself in the slip of my hips
& now she lives in all the mirrors
of my apartment.
now she pats me on the belly
& begs for me to feed her.
so i search me out some rood boys,
those thick two-headed ox-men.
cook me up some fine soup,
roast sweet potatoes on parchment,
then i sucks me down them oxtails!
girl, i cost them!
#hallelujah to the HoodWitches.
to the snapbacks & double daps
of qweens gone pedestrian.
#blessedbe to they children's children.
may the gawds smile down
& watch over the black naps
& snatched backs of black womxn
dragged into the system. of black
womxn survived outside the system. black
womxn survived despite the system. #asheashe

to my black girls gone missing.
to my sisters gone missing.
to our daughters & granddaughters.
to our mamas & grandmamas.
#asheashe to the crowned & uncrowned

to those
above
&
below
ground.

notes

ABOUT SECTION TITLE PAGES

The First Rite of Water: The image is a veve of Papa Legba, a loa in Haitian Vodou. He is often invoked when humans try to connect with the spirits, and can give or deny permission to speak with the gods.

The Second Rite of Flesh: The image is a veve of Maman Brigitte, a death loa in Haitian Vodou.

The Third Rite of Smoke: The image is a veve of Baron Samedi, a death loa in Haitian Vodou.

ABOUT THE POEMS

The final section of "About the Girl Who Would Become a Gawd" includes binary code that translates to "Say Her Name, Say My Name."

"Photo of X, 2003: Abstractions" contains binary code that translates to "I am god."

"Photo of X, 2004: Fish with Yemayá": Yemayá is an Orisha from the Yoruba tradition, a mother figure and a water deity.

"Photo of a Girl, 1994: Gawd": In the Bible, Samson loses his strength when his hair is cut by Delilah.

"whoever." is a poem designed after Rumi's translated line, "Whoever brought me here will have to take me home."

"Hex for R. Kelly" is written after an actual hex found in *The Voodoo Hoodoo Spellbook* by Denise Alvarado. The original hex can be found on page 259 of the text, under "The Curse of Marie Laveau."

"The Daughters of Samuel Little": In 2014, Samuel Little was convicted for the murder of three women, but he has since been linked to approximately thirty-four murders and has confessed to as many as ninety.

"Concrete Qweens": In 2014, rapper Juicy J offered a $50,000 scholarship to "the best chick who can twerk." After reading the rules, single mother Zaire Holmes submitted a video that did NOT show her twerking and walked away with the grand prize.

"Photo of X, 2005: What Dreams Are These?" is written after Allen Ginsberg's "Howl."

"Saint She of All the Missing Things" is styled after Sylvia Plath's collection *Ariel*.

"Year of the Dog" is written for Freddie Gray, who went into a coma after a spinal fracture incurred during his short trip to the police station in the back of a van. Section 4 of this poem references a lyric from a song by Hip Hop artist Jibbs called "Chain Hang Low".

"For the White Girl in Poetry Workshop Who Says I Don't Belong Here": The digitus medius is the middle finger, which is also the number four when you count the binary code by hand.

GLOSSARY OF TERMS

Brick dust: Used in protection spells, normally in regard to protecting one's home.
Florida Water: Used for spiritual cleansing and protection of the home.
Womxn: Including women from all origins.
Blxck: Including those from mixed backgrounds.

acknowledgments

To the editors and staff members of the following publications: You make it a little easier for writers like myself to dream. I thank you for all of the work that you do and for accepting early versions of the poems included in this collection:

American Poetry Journal, The Cincinnati Review, Cosmonauts Avenue, Five:2:One Magazine, Foundry Journal, Glass Poetry Press, Ink & Nebula, Kweli Journal, Lunch Ticket Journal, The Matador Review, Pidgeonholes, Poetry Magazine, the Prairie Schooner Literary Journal, The Rockvale Review, The Rumpus, Tahoma Literary Review, and Yes Poetry Magazine.

I want to thank the astounding team at Acre Books, especially my editors Lisa Ampleman and Nicola Mason, who trusted my vision and worked so hard to help me bring it forth, and my cover designer, Barbara Bourgoyne, for her excellent work.

Thank you to Tyrone Geter for allowing me to use such a powerful piece of original art to introduce my work to the world. When I first saw the image, I was disturbed by how much it resembled myself. It is the self I have spent many years trying to hide from others, the dangerous and disturbed side of myself. But like the book itself, it has forced me to embrace the things that have scared me the most and given me great joy.

There are so many names I want to herald here. To those who have let me sleep on their couches when I was without a home, those who have given me food and drink when I was hungry, those who have held me together while I was falling apart, those who have loved me despite my faults, those who have trusted me with their time or money or hearts, those who have guided me through my failures, those who have supported me as an artist and as a sister and as a friend—thank you. I will never be able to say it enough. Thank you.

I want to thank the following groups for raising me up when I felt I was falling:

Austin Neo Soul, I will never forget the night you shut the venue down to hold me as a family after Ray's death; Austin Poetry Slam for birthing me as a poet; Grid Squid Entertainment for being both my family and my friends; The Dream Team, Gamma Sigma Sigma National Service Sorority for giving me some of the best years of my young life; Sierra Nevada College's MFA Program for restoring my faith in the power of the written word; Splash Coworking and Open Mouth Writing Retreat for helping find myself as an artist—again.

I want to thank the following people, who have served as mentors and friends, sisters and brothers, lights and visionaries: Troy Baham Jr., Jessica Hamilton, Alison Papion, Shanneen Harris, Billy Tuggle, Candyce Tuggle, Brian Francis, Michelle Desiree, Stacie Shea, Carina Pinales, Pari Sandage, Cyrus Cassells, Laura Wetherington, Patricia Smith, Brian Turner, Lee Herrick, Carolyn Forché, Jonnie Wilson, Daniel Gamez, Kyra Hicks, Wendy Hill, Gretchen Boulaine, Jerome Hayes, Jerome Horton, and Airea D. Matthews.

I want to thank my father, Aubrey Hicks. I am so grateful to you for all that you have given to make my life possible. I want to thank my sisters, Katrina Kinds, Shamika Hicks, and Katonya Hicks. I love you all so much that it hurts sometimes. I would never have worked as hard if it weren't for all of you. I want to thank my mother, Linda Gamez. I am grateful for all that you have done to ensure that love was a constant in our lives. I survived this long only because you taught me how to.

I want to thank Carz. In person. One day. And I want to thank my ancestors. I call them now, with respect and humility, to thank them for their guidance and for their love. I call them now, with honor and appreciation, knowing that they are always with me.

Ray Allen Courtney Jr.
Ray Allen Courtney
Gabrielle Bouliane
Sheila Siobhan
Shannon Leigh Lewis
Anita Hicks
Lucille McNeese
Earl Mosley Jr.
LDB III
Wayne Hicks
Rita Marie Gamez

And every single black girl gone missing.